Spiritual Musings

Spiritual Musings

by

Frederick Castor

Edie

you have always been

an inspiration to me

Cover design by Steve Hays
www.fort-collins-graphic-design.com

Interior design by Jennifer Top
www.jennifertop.com

To my family

Contents

Acknowledgments

Thanks primarily to my wife, Robin, for putting up with me during this process, for invaluable technological assistance, and for caring enough to play devil's advocate, thereby preventing me from making serious mistakes.

Thanks also to the following: my daughters, Jane O'Leary and Claire Gilliland, for their abundant support of my writing; my son, Jeremy, and his wife, Jenn, for their help in choosing a title and deciding on the cover design; Doug Anderson for his enduring friendship and constant support; Don Imsland for thoughtfully leading me through the maze of title choices; Wanda Knauer for her interest, support, and input in deciding on a title and cover design; Dave O'Brien for his excitement, for editing my script, and for his written comments; Steve Hays for his patience with me while designing the cover; Sandi Ohlen for her encouragement and written comments;

Linda Bobbitt for her long-term support and written comments; Bill Brown for his gracious written comments; Brad Runyan for his kind written words; and Jennifer Top for editing my script and formatting it for publication.

Introduction to Spiritual Musings

Spirituality has been around since the beginning of time. The creation story in the Bible attempts to reveal God's creating humanity (however that occurred) for the sole purpose of having an engaging relationship with someone. That engagement between God and humans was a spiritual one—God being Spirit.

Although that early relationship was disrupted because of human arrogance, God has been quite busy ever since, reaching out, attempting to restore that spiritual connection (Moses, the kings of Israel and Judah, the Old Testament prophets). History records the countless individuals who have responded to God's welcoming invitation. We are among them.

The average Christian is likely unaware of the many outstanding individuals during the last few centuries who have written and taught, sharing the spiritual nature of their faith.

Spirituality has been enmeshed in religious history ever since history has been recorded. Within the last few centuries spirituality has risen as a *rising sun* within various religious communities, including the Christian Church—illuminating God's original plan.

History clearly discloses the Church has been at its best when it has kept at front and center the spiritual nature of its engagement with God. The more judiciously that relationship has been maintained, the more dynamic the Church has been. However, the Church has strayed and often lost its way when other causes have been allowed to invade and alter the central position of the spiritual connection and interaction with God. It has at particular times become idolatrous.

For that reason, many individuals have forsaken the Church, saying it has lost its Spirit. Many people today claim they are not religious because organized religion no longer speaks to them. Yet, they still claim to be spiritual—connected to God—that critical dimension of faith.

This reality can be measured by the decline in worship attendance, resulting in the closing of a frightening number of Christian churches, particularly in North America and Europe. However, understand this phenomenon is not universal. The Church is alive and well in some parts of the world, e.g., Central and South America and the Far East. Notably, the Churches in those areas are quite spiritual in their orientation and modus operandi.

The above-described landscape is the backdrop for *Spiritual Musings*. The following essays are written, first, for those people who are not inspired by what goes on in the Church and decidedly do not participate, who nevertheless see themselves as being spiritual but not religious. *Spiritual Musings* is also written for the many people within the Christian Church who yearn for more than they are experiencing.

It is always a huge challenge for the Church to move away from the many distractions that plague it and back to its spiritual base in order to fulfill its designated mission.

All of this can occur if we, as individuals and the Church, focus sharply on enhancing and energizing our personal and corporate relationship with the Holy One—the essence of spirituality.

Differentiating Spirituality from Religion

The following thoughts are shared to help readers appreciate the unique quality of spirituality and the profound opportunity of embarking upon a spiritual journey as the most meaningful way to orient and live life. A life imbued with a spiritual orientation is endowed with a unique quality.

While any effort to differentiate spirituality from religion is simplistic, it is nevertheless a helpful place to begin and is useful in designating the trailhead from which to embark upon a spiritual journey.

The term *spiritual* often gets used to describe practices and activities that clearly are not spiritual but strictly religious in nature. It is not always easy to differentiate spiritual qualities from religious activities although they are two very different phenomena. They are closely related, frequently appearing together, yet they are two totally different experiences and represent two divergent orientations toward God.

An increasing number of individuals are now saying they are spiritual but not religious. As noted in the Introduction, there are many reasons for this stance. The effect of this thought process is that people are finding ways to encounter and relate to God that do not involve worshiping in a community. Only they know how satisfying and helpful that orientation is.

On the other hand, there are many people who practice religion with intense fervor within a worshiping community who miss the joy of a spiritual life without ever understanding why. They only know their religious practice does not satisfy their deepest yearning. Consequently, many people give up on their religious practices because these practices do not quench their spiritual thirst.

There are also people who are disappointed in their religious lives, who work even harder at their religious practices in hopes they can squeeze from them something that brings that inner peace for which they yearn. Unfortunately, it never happens because peace is not the product of our religious efforts and pursuits, but a spiritual gift. Religion is not designed to produce peace but to engage us in useful and constructive activity as God's people. Peace is a gift that comes from our engagement with God.

Religion is in part observable action people carry out in the forms of worship, caring behavior, and compassion, among other exercises. These are the things religious people have done and feel compelled to do because they are considered to be God-like or God-pleasing acts. There is a historical record of people having done them ad infinitum. Scripture is full of such actions, and it calls us all to such action. Religious Christians might speak of the *Christian thing to do.*

Religion can also be expressed in systems of belief such as Jewish, Islamic, or Christian teachings. These systems of belief vary from one religious group to another and unfortunately create *exclusive* communities rather than *inclusive* ones.

In this writing, *spirituality* is understood to be that connection with God who is personal, immediately present to us in our world and within our personal lives. A spiritual experience is one in which God's Spirit engages and nourishes our spirits—the ultimate human experience. A spiritual life is one that is in a growing relationship with God, one in which a person seeks to allow God to enter one's life and become a true partner assisting with life's struggles and celebrating life's successes. Thus, a spiritual life can become a life engaged significantly with God even to the point of surrender. Surrender is not generally considered to be a positive act. However, surrender to God is the ultimate act we can perform.

This inner engagement with God is mysterious and not outwardly observable as are traditional religious activities. However, when out of this unique relationship certain actions of compassion and behavioral change begin to occur, these expressions of spirituality become religious actions and are then observable. When a religious expression or activity emerges from a spiritual experience with God and becomes observable by others, it also becomes repeatable. It can be taught and passed on from one generation to another. It can be held up as a worthwhile model and used to train people to repeat a particular behavior. When such behavior is carried out in practice, because of its obvious worth to society and its being done in the name of God, it is religion. The familiar golden rule, *Do unto others as you would have them do unto you,* is a classic example of teachable religious behavior.

The irony is that one can actually be involved in religious practice that is compassionate, loving, and generous all in the name of God, but unless he or she also has that inner spiritual connection to God, the religious practice in and of itself can be hollow.

Spirituality is that essence of our relationship with God that is initially created solely by the Holy Spirit who calls us into a life-giving relationship and energizes every dimension of our lives. The difference between spirituality and religion can also be understood by noting that religion can be *taught* by one generation to another while spirituality must be *caught* one individual at a time. It is a personal transformation experience in which the Holy Spirit connects us to the Holy One and alters our innermost being, which is different from assimilating information about God and/or the acting out of specific behavioral patterns.

The Spirit of God who lives within all of us, whether or not we recognize it, is about the business of connecting us to God and transforming us from within to become new creatures. It is an exciting metamorphosis that from the outside can be invisible, but from the inside is a powerful, joyful, and peace-giving experience. It is a fantastic journey well worth pursuing.

Buying into the Spiritual World

C. S. Lewis's book *The Lion, the Witch and the Wardrobe* is a wonderful although frightening fantasy, which, as all fantasies, points to a reality that can scarcely be described in ordinary terms. Lewis's fantasy tells of characters passing through a wardrobe into a totally different world of reality.

There is a spiritual world running parallel to the physical world, often intertwined with it, and we live in both simultaneously. Unfortunately, we spend most of our time paying attention to the physical world and are oblivious to the spiritual world in which we also live.

According to the Biblical account, the spiritual world, including God, existed prior to the physical world God called into being. Having been created in the image of God, we are born with a spiritual component along with our physical faculties. This allows us to participate in that parallel life of the spirit as we live our physical lives. It is unquestionably evident that there is far more to us than the physical bodies we see reflected in a mirror.

There are two points that need to be made at this juncture. First, the world of the spirit is as real as the physical world. If this were not true, then there could be no God because God *is* spirit. Second, being created as we are, we are equipped to participate in both worlds.

There are special properties that spiritual entities possess. The most common one, from a human perspective, is this: Things of the spirit normally are invisible to us because our vision is limited to perceiving only the physical. However, available to our physical vision are the *effects* of the Spirit's activity.

The Greek word for spirit is *pneuma,* translated as *air* or *wind,* and it is the root of the familiar words pneumonia and pneumatic. We cannot see air or wind, but we are very aware of their effects upon the physical world. We cannot visually perceive God who is spirit, but we can become aware of what God has done and continues to do in our world and in our own lives—the effects of His presence and activity.

As we investigate the spiritual world, we discover there is a larger reality lying behind and beyond our physical world—a spiritual world—in which we can participate. In this spiritual world we encounter and get to know the Holy Other.

On the Day of Pentecost, the presence of the Holy Other was manifested in the rushing winds and flames as of fire. People of different nations who spoke different languages were mysteriously able to understand each other. On that day the world of the Spirit broke into the physical world in a miraculous way.

We can illustrate the difference between the typical, but valuable, religious experience and the spiritual experience by considering the difference between snorkeling and scuba diving. Snorkeling gives us glimpses beneath the surface of the sea. We can see beautiful coral formations and exotic fish with their bright colors. Scuba diving, on the other hand, gives us a different perspective and allows us to become immediately involved in the mysteries of the sea.

Our typical religious experience is closer to snorkeling when we look from a distance with only a glimpse of the Holy Other. The spiritual experience, on the other hand, engages us immediately in the realities of the Holy Other world.

The spiritual journey is living in this physical world while intentionally engaging in the Wholly Other world of God's Spirit.

The Impossible God

We have been created with rational minds. We have been given the ability to think, reason, evaluate, and discern. Our minds are incredible, enabling us to survive and thrive in our challenging world. As wonderful as it is for us to have rational, creative minds, it is ironic that we use them to apply reason to our perception of God. In so doing we find ourselves placing limits on what we think God is capable of doing. For example: How can God be personally engaged with every person on earth? How can God possibly hear and respond to the millions of prayers that are offered simultaneously? According to reason, it cannot be. In fact, according to reason there cannot even be a God.

We cannot reasonably prove God even exists, but neither can we prove God does not exist. That perhaps is the key. There are some things lying beyond reason—God being one.

From the perspective of human reason, God is impossible. Yet, we know from experience God does exist, is real, and has through self-revelation become known to us. Thus, that which exceeds the reaches of human reason can be and is in existence in the person of God.

If we get over the initial hump and concede God does exist, it opens to us unlimited possibilities and potential. We can accept the idea that God can reveal to us the very nature of the Divine.

It is at this juncture that confusion begins to arise. It has been said a little knowledge is dangerous. That certainly applies here. God has revealed limited knowledge to us. We have taken this limited knowledge, mistakenly assumed it is complete, and ascribed to this Divine being all sorts of qualities, each assortment in turn creating a devout following. This has resulted in myriad religious groupings, each claiming ultimate authenticity.

Once reason, with its voice of authority, is suspended, allowing for the existence of God, nothing is beyond imagination, including false conclusions and mistaken beliefs.

That is precisely why committing to a particular belief system has its hazards. However authentic it promises to be, it is still subject to error because God appears to have chosen to reveal only limited knowledge, leaving the rest to faith.

What, then, can we trust? Our best bet is to lay to rest our efforts to understand God's modus operandi and spend our time and effort enhancing our relationship with the Holy One. Let God prove Divine viability. Let God reveal to us what we are to know—including limits to our knowing.

Understanding fully the nature of God is far beyond our ability. God seems to have let us in on all we need to understand about the Divine plan. The basic plan is that we are designed to be in a meaningful relationship with the Holy One as children of a loving parent.

It isn't *comprehension* God wants from us. It is a *relationship* with us that rises above all else in importance, as mysterious as it might seem.

The God in Whom We Live and Move and Have Our Being

Consciously living and moving and having our being in God is the most rewarding way there is to live. There is nothing more we can do to enhance our relationship with the Holy One beyond this awareness. It is not a matter of obedience or belief. Rather, it is living enshrouded by God's very Being. Nothing can be more meaningful than this incomparable lifestyle.

Our awareness of this tight connection, and acting upon it, drastically alters our perception of everything in our lives. It changes the way we see ourselves, all of our relationships, our purpose in life, and our behavior. Life becomes less stressful, giving us a profound sense of peace.

Living with an awareness that our very being is encompassed within God's holy presence is truly incomprehensible. In this incredible circumstance we are beyond incredulity. None of our senses are capable of measuring the sheer intensity and the amazing effect of this phenomenon.

The fact is, this condition always exists as a function of God's ever present love for us. It is constant—omnipresent. Our cognizance of the existing condition is what makes the ultimate difference. This is the function of inspiration, adjusting our awareness so this phenomenon is never out of focus but clearly apparent.

It is bountifully comforting to experience the effects of this reality invading our consciousness and informing the citadel of our wills of this magnanimous gift. We live and move and have our being in Almighty God! It is holy to its core, beyond all description.

It makes a more radical difference in everything we do than anything else in our lives, if we only allow its leaven to work in our thoughts and actions.

It is already in place. It requires nothing more of us than to acknowledge it and commit to living our lives within its field of energy.

The difference it makes is magical! A newness breaks out as the sun breaks through the storm clouds. A profound peace engulfs our lives. It has the taste of heaven.

Engaging with God

Much has been said and written about God's presence. People of faith are aware that God is present in their lives, guiding and protecting them. Likewise, there is an awareness that God is present and operative in the world in general—CEO of maintenance.

We are abundantly blessed to have God present in our lives. It makes an unbelievable difference. As we look around we can see how God has changed the lives of countless people— hopefully our own. Truly God is omnipresent and active.

As magnanimous as it is to live in God's holy presence, there is something even more exquisite. One step further is open to us beyond being aware of God's presence. It is becoming engaged with God. We might envision an infant child nursing at its mother's breast. Nourishment is immediately transmitted, bringing sustenance to the infant. Beyond the actual nourishment there lies a profound spiritual connection between mother and child—one that has deep roots and huge benefits. Much more is occurring than the mere transmission of physical nourishment—something that awakens the innermost core of both the mother and the child. There is a spiritual bond like no other in human life.

It is that sort of spiritual bond we can have with God. It is a relationship in which there is mutual benefit. Not only are we beneficiaries of a cartload of blessings; God is also being satisfied by our connection—as a mother nursing her child.

We are inevitably puzzled by God's presence and greatness. We cannot begin to comprehend this awesome reality. How there can even be a God escapes our elementary understanding. There is a vast gap between God and us. While it is a chasm we cannot cross, it is nevertheless one God has been relentlessly crossing in order to engage us.

From the beginning of time God has sought us out in order to have a meaningful relationship with us and showered us with immeasurable gifts of love and mercy. We are constantly being coddled.

Being engaged with God in this sort of closeness is God's intent and purpose. For our part we need only to desire it and be open to this awesome opportunity. It is as close to heaven as we can get while remaining on this earth.

God lets us grow, develop, work, and play, but no experience in life, however exalted, exceeds the fullness and tenderness of our awesome engagement with the Holy One.

A Spiritual Journey—An Incomparable Faith Experience

The spiritual journey is a matter of getting to know God more fully and allowing the Holy Spirit to give new life and energy to dormant, if not dead, religious practice.

It is very easy for even the best religious practices to lose their vitality. For example, praying the Lord's Prayer can be a powerful, spiritual, life-changing experience, or it can become a powerless practice. We use it often in worship services so the words are quite familiar. How often have we merely slid over the words without even considering the radical nature of praying *Thy will be done?*

This prayerful statement is radical because the petition asks that our wills be put into sync with God's will. That may sound like a good idea initially, but we should consider that our wills at that moment may be 180 degrees apart from God's will, and on an entirely different mission. Is that what we truly mean to ask at that moment when we slide over the words so thoughtlessly? We need to be crystal clear about what we ask of God.

This journey, like any journey, calls for careful planning and deliberate action, in this case seeking God's Spirit to give vitality, meaning, and understanding to this unique experience. This journey begins by recognizing what has always been and is always true, namely, all things are under God's control. We need to accept that truism, celebrate it, and most of all capitalize on this amazing reality. If God is in control, the pressure is off us. What a relief that awareness should bring. We are free to live fully and actually do God's will.

Pursuing a spiritual journey teaches us to live every dimension of life under the direction and protection of God's Holy Spirit. But as with learning to ski, swim, drive, or ride a bicycle, we can talk about it, watch videos about it, or think about it forever, with no results. We do not learn to do it until we actually embark. Thankfully, God has equipped us for this task. We just need to get started and stick with it.

The tools we need and have readily available to us are prayer, quiet time, listening to God, and making room for God to plant thoughts in our minds. Our prayers do not have to be elaborate or even correct by some standard. They can be mere passing thoughts that we share quietly with the Holy One, or they can be extensive and well-thought-out ideas. That which is important is to do whatever the Spirit moves us to do. We are on a spiritual journey when we begin to trust God's Spirit to lead and direct us on a daily basis.

Quiet time with acute awareness of being in God's Holy presence is a requisite and represents a most essential tool. It is perhaps the most difficult one we must learn to use.

Truly, a spiritual journey guided and inspired by God's Holy Spirit is an incomparable faith experience.

Prayer: The Great Connector, the Exquisite Mystery

It should be obvious, prayer is the primary means of connecting with God. Basic communication is the key to developing any relationship. Speaking, listening, and sharing are the elements that constitute communication and underlie the building of healthy relationships. When we do this with God we call it prayer. The stakes are highest when we communicate with God in prayer.

Although it follows the same general principle as any meaningful conversation, prayer is unique because of the nature of the person to whom it is addressed, and with whom it is pursued. While prayer can assume many valid forms, it always constitutes the soaring of the human spirit to meet and engage God's Spirit. Thus, prayer is *the great connector.*

Because of its potential, it is of utmost importance we pause and recognize each of the dimensions of prayer. Prayer is an *exquisite mystery* for several reasons. There is nothing that comes even close to the energy that is present in entering into God's Holy Presence—a most amazing energy field. As powerful as the word *exquisite* is, it cannot begin to convey the specialness of communicating with the Holy One. Merely being in God's Presence is so powerful in itself, but additionally to share a conversation with Almighty God goes beyond anything we can imagine.

Prayer is also mysterious. How can we communicate with a spirit? How can God communicate with so many millions of people at once and respond in meaningful ways? Prayer makes no sense from the stance of reason. Yet, we find ourselves praying, and we are awed and grateful when our prayers are answered!

How it all takes place baffles our sense of reason. Yet, when we become engaged with God in prayer, however clumsily our efforts might be, something happens. Prayer changes things! If we persist, perhaps in spite of our skepticism, changes begin to occur within us. Life takes on a different hue. The circumstances we pray to have changed may also change. Our prayer may well become a matter of asking God to enter into the scene and work the wonders that are beyond our control. This is child's play for God. The process is primarily one of asking God to enter into the situation and make whatever difference needs to be made.

The beauty of a prayerful life is the ultimate difference it makes within this exquisite and mysterious relationship we have with the Holy One. The way God answers our prayers is all a bonus. The primary value of prayer is in the spiritual energy it generates.

Listening for God's Message

Some people appear gifted with the ability to hear and recognize God's relating a message to them. Others struggle with varying degrees of success and often are left with severe disappointment over their inability to receive what God is trying to tell them. Still others totally dismiss the idea of God's communicating with anyone in any such direct manner. If one is lacking in experience in this arena, it is understandable that doubt and dismissal occur.

It is unfortunate that, for whatever reason, many people are lacking this inspiring experience. However, there is much evidence of communication encounters that account for iconic things such as Holy Scripture, palpable evidence of God's communication schematic.

There are many reasons why God's messages to us are missed. The one main reason is we have not yet learned what to expect and, therefore, have not trained ourselves to be receptive. The intent of this document is to restate the possibility available to us and suggest ways to capitalize on this unique opportunity. God does send us messages; we can learn to receive them. The way this happens is to train our receptors—dialing them to the correct frequency. When we learn how to do this, the signal—messages—begin to come through.

The one basic requirement for successfully receiving these divinely originated messages is to clear our minds of the din and chaff constantly occupying our conscious attention. We must get a handle on our roaming thoughts and consciously put them on the back burner for a time. We must deliberately take control of our meandering thoughts and dismiss them for a time in order to make way for God's messages to come through.

This can be done only with God's help, which becomes our prayer: *Clear my mind, Holy One, and make way for your message to me.* Visualize being alone with God. This requires engaging our imagination, which, once in this arena, we can allow to run freely. We can sense God's presence at least to some degree, knowing that God is always present to us. *Awaken my spiritual sensors to enable me to become aware of your presence. Sensitize my spirit so I am able to receive and recognize your message to me.*

It is an awesome moment to move into this place; it is indeed the Holy of Holies. Yet, the process is no different from learning most other things in which we wish to become proficient. We learn to walk; we learn to talk; we learn to type; we learn to drive; we learn to swim; we learn to ski. We can also learn to recognize God's messages if we commit ourselves to this learning process. Of all things we can learn to do to enrich our lives, this ability will prove to make the greatest difference.

Where and how might these messages from God appear? How can we prompt ourselves to be discerning? God's messages to us can come at any time and in countless forms. God sometimes simply puts his thoughts into our minds. We begin thinking about what God has to say to us. Also, God speaks to us in the words of other people, scripture, songs, hymns, liturgy, and ordinary conversations. The sources are limitless and often startling.

The cue is always that we hear, see, or imagine something standing out like a four-leaf clover in a clover patch. For a God-given reason, we are brought up short and miraculously made aware that this is from God. When this happens, stop on the spot and be quiet. *Here am I, Holy One, speak to me and I will hear you.*

Quiet Time: Life's Most Lucrative Investment

Investments are an important part of our portfolios, intended to increase the value of our estates, often with an eye toward retirement. Not all investments are productive. Poor ones can be quite costly. Then there are the omnipresent scams that are totally destructive. They promise unbelievably high returns, but, alas, produce only total loss. We are often warned that if something seems too good to be true, it probably is just that— not true.

There is one offer that is true and not a scam. It is life's most lucrative investment—quiet time. Invest in quiet time. Invest in time set apart from daily routine and busyness. The minutes of our days are poker chips on the table. We have X number of them, and the challenge is to convert those minutes into something that has the greatest value—something that has maximum return.

There is nothing in which we can invest our minutes that produces anything close to the increased value that quiet time produces. Using these special moments to pray and meditate is a most creative investment. We should use this time to share with God our concerns as well as offering thanks. Quiet time is the time to listen to that *still small voice of God* within us.

This phenomenon of hearing God speak has a long and credible history that appears throughout scripture. In fact, from a spiritual perspective, that is the greatest value of scripture—recording the experiences of various individuals in human history who have been able to hear and discern God speaking to them. That is the experience we wish to replicate here and now in our lives— listening to God speak to us. Time, attention, and effort spent listening to God speak to us are life's most lucrative investment.

The way to invest is with your time—your minutes available during the day or night. Most people feel there are no extra minutes available during the day. The days are full! Every minute is filled to the brim. Not one is free or open.

How have we acquired that crowded schedule? A better question would be, Why have we created that lifestyle? It is a function of our latent desire to be in control of our lives and be successful. Unfortunately, the result is the exact opposite of our desire—a total loss of control. Life gets out of control. The demands we place on our time and allow to fill our minutes take control of us.

What this does to our time—our minutes—is to reduce their value because we have invested in a scam that seeks to take from us the value of our investment. Incessant busyness is a monumental scam.

The only way out of this morass is to begin investing in something better, something more productive, something of greater value. Busyness is not a blue chip. It is a loser. It is like quicksand because it is so very difficult to extricate ourselves from its grip. It sucks us in. Busyness is truly demonic, and to succumb to its power is not a hallmark of success but of failure.

We need to invest some of our precious minutes in quiet time—prayer and meditation. This is a most worthwhile way to extricate ourselves from the quagmire of busyness. This is the resource God has provided and invites us to use. Quiet time spent with the Holy One is down time, time in which we emotionally and consciously shift our awareness into a spiritual sphere. In so doing we become aware we are in a different dimension of reality. We are in fact in God's immediate presence where God's thoughts become our thoughts.

When in these precious moments our minds become quiet, we can begin to listen. We listen for anything God puts into our consciousness—any thought that bears God's signature.

At this juncture in our quiet time we must employ the power of the Holy Spirit who becomes God's voice to us. The Holy

Spirit is a fabulous teacher and, perhaps best of all, lives with us at all times. We are never left alone to discern and interpret God's messages. Ever the teacher, the Holy Spirit comes alive within us and enables us to recognize messages as coming from God versus extraneous and devious thoughts that flash on the screen of our awareness. The Holy Spirit leads us gently through the maze of thoughts coming to us in these special moments of quiet receptivity, identifying which ones come from God and which ones do not.

At this point in our quiet time, we need simply to relax and let it happen. Having made the conscious effort to claim these quiet moments for spiritual renewal, we need not exert any further effort at this point. We merely relax and enjoy the fact we are in a different time frame and a different sphere of awareness.

We listen. Quietly we listen. Expectantly we listen. It is truly a phenomenal experience. It awakens our spirits with vitality and richness beyond belief. The best! Special minutes with the Holy One are life's most lucrative investment. There is no more efficient way of getting to know God better than to be quiet and listen to what God mixes into our thoughts.

Basking in God's Presence

Awareness of being in God's presence is a very special gift and one not experienced universally. Unfortunately, there are many profoundly spiritual people who deeply desire this awareness but for some reason are unable to have this unique experience. Apparently, God has doled out special gifts to specific people. The reason for this selectivity is unknown to us.

It is clear, however, that awareness of being in God's immediate presence is a special gift. Yet, just because a person has until now not received this gift, it is no reason to believe one cannot receive it in the future. As is true with all things coming from God, the key is in our desire and prayerful, persistent request. As is also true, there are times we ask God for something special and we get something different—but better. That is quite common. The gift of awareness of being in God's presence remains our focus. It stands out as a mountain top experience and is highly desirable.

It is imperative to differentiate between *being in God's presence* and *being aware of being in God's presence*. The fact is, we are constantly in God's presence, which is a blessing of untold value in itself. However, awareness of being in God's presence is a whole different gift and is the ultimate experience.

This awareness radicalizes our lives, giving them deeper meaning. It becomes the stage on which everything else in our day gets acted out. It is the backdrop of every act, the prop that accentuates every action, the energy that motivates us in everything we do. It transforms the way we perceive everything and makes us glow.

As we become more aware that our lives are lived in God's awesome presence, the initial sprig of joy grows bountifully and blossoms. It is truly awesome, adding another dimension to our lives and in full color.

Living in God's presence is like walking in the sun. Awareness of being in God's presence is like basking in the sun. It is transcendent!

Maintaining Spiritual Awareness

The goal of maintaining *spiritual awareness,* while challenging, is attainable, once we decide in our hearts it is something we truly desire. It is this initial desire that we must wrestle with until we are quite clear that this dimension of our lives is important enough to claim our time and attention. This desire must be unequivocal.

It does not require that we give up other important facets of our lives, but we do learn to perceive all of life as a spiritual journey with everything in life being *colored spiritual.*

We do not live a spiritual life by only doing spiritual things from time to time. Rather, we are made aware because life is a gift from God; all of life is meant to have a spiritual flavor. It is this unique awareness that enables us to enjoy a deeper relationship with God. Eventually, this awareness changes everything about us and affects everything we do and how we do it. It gives us a new lease on life and useful handles for living it more fully.

Maintaining spiritual consciousness is a matter of attitude. It is an ongoing perceptual-adjusting process, a continual refocusing. In retrospect we will begin to realize, *I am different. I view things differently. My attitude is more positive. I am more caring. My life is more joyful.* A newness and freshness emerge.

Our role in this life-changing process is first the *desire*, then giving it time and attention, and finally, waiting patiently for God to make it happen.

Following are some suggestions for maintaining spiritual awareness throughout each day. It is the day after day practice that nourishes and enhances our relationship with God, which is the goal of our spiritual journey. It should and can become habitual.

Think of the purpose of the Sabbath in the original creation and how important it is to rest and pray.

Look upon moments with God as gifts rather than obligations.

Have a prayer agenda that encourages you to talk to God about the next day.

After your special time with God, write down what you experienced during those moments to reinforce its value in your mind so you will be inclined to do it again. Keep a journal and read it occasionally. It will document the growth as well as the weak spots.

Read the words of Psalms to activate those spiritual juices. Read until some specific thought snares your attention. Carry that thought throughout the day. Do the same with this book.

Begin every day with the awareness that it will be spent with God regardless of having that awareness fade as the day progresses. *O Holy One, thank you for inviting me into YOUR day so I can have the joy of being with you in everything I do.*

Steal moments throughout the day to breathe deeply six times, and relax your shoulders and neck, thanking God for each breath.

Whenever you participate in corporate worship, listen for a single word, sentence, or thought that stands out and catches your attention. Write it down. Tape it to the dashboard of your car (keep a roll of tape in your car). Ponder it briefly each time you start your car.

Always use red traffic lights and railroad crossing delays for deep breathing, relaxing, and a quick prayer of gratitude.

Throughout each day thank God for every good thing that occurs, and invite God in to share with you everything tough, trying, or painful. Prayerfully include God in whatever you are experiencing, however unimportant it might be.

Thank God for any guilt you feel because it is a lifesaving

hook God uses to rescue you. After dealing with the issue with God, let it go.

Choose one person for whom you will pray throughout each day—someone in need, a friend, a world leader. Intercessory prayer has invaluable potency.

Don't try everything at once. Add another practice into your daily routine only after your first practice becomes established and stable.

Keep a bookmark at this place for quick regular reference.

The Peace of God That Passes All Understanding

The peace that comes from knowing God is all encompassing—so remarkable that one hardly knows how to begin describing it. Indeed, it does defy our understanding. It exceeds our ability to comprehend its magnanimity. When it comes, it prevails over all other feelings we have and is truly overwhelming.

The late Dr. Joseph Sittler, a renowned twentieth-century theologian, wrote of two dimensions of peace. "On the one hand, peace is a most desirable personal state of well-being. It is 'rest' from the turmoil of personal living in a turbulent society and conflicted world."

In this sense, peace is a gift from God that enables us to live above the din that oppresses us and to transcend the stresses, trials, and struggles of life. God's gift of peace lifts us out of the reach of these tentacles, keeping us safe. Our spirits can be at rest rather than distraught. This restful peace in the midst of turmoil is truly a spiritual gift. Because of God's mysterious grace it is available to us for the asking.

The second dimension of peace, according to Sittler, is the extension of this personal peace. "It is an active outreach into our homes, societies and entire world, extending that same transcendent gift—that sense of well-being—to all people." It was this gift of which the angel spoke: "Peace on earth and good will among all people." Peace is more than a pleasant concept, it is a potent power that issues from God and affects relationships throughout the world.

We definitely live in a most imperfect world where peace is rare. Conflict and discord abound. Strife reigns in many quarters. Nations threaten each other. Natural and human disasters occur almost universally. Our own society is freighted with stress-producing incidents. Our very way of life is pressurized to the point of explosion, which does occur with high frequency in the form of damaging threats to our health, disruption of interpersonal relationships, horrible mass shootings, and war. Marriage dissolution has become the norm. Overall the scene is depressing and frightening.

Where is God's peace in the midst of this tumultuous scene? It seems almost an insult to our intelligence to peddle God's peace in the presence of this pugnacious caldron of discord. Alas, so many people miss a golden opportunity for *peace* because they cannot maintain even a sliver of hope in this threatening morass.

The folly of taking a defeated stance, in the midst of this admittedly threatening onslaught, is that it fails to account for God's involvement and power. It dismisses God without reckoning with the divine promises that are made squarely in the face of seemingly omnipresent despair.

The world has forever been in this disarray to some degree. The presence of evil must be acknowledged. It is not a Pollyanna scene.

However, it is over and against this very scene and reality that God promises *peace.* Squarely in the midst of all hate and disruptions *God's peace* dares to enter and change the scene with a peace that escapes all human understanding. We cannot begin to grasp this possibility. Yet, we can receive this peace into our lives and experience its settling effect within our being, even while the world around us roils in conflict and our own lives are violently shaken. God's peace is nothing short of a miracle. There is no other way of explaining it. It goes against all rational odds. Yet, while we cannot understand or explain this amazing peace, we can definitely experience it and in turn share it in whatever way opportunities present themselves.

It must be clearly stated that this is not a flight from reality but an incredible gift of an even greater reality. It comes with a deep sense of knowing God and learning to live in this Holy Presence. It divests us of a fear that apart from this close connection would inevitably prevail as it does constantly all around us. We can become an island of peace in the churning sea of greed—an oasis of calm in a desert of lust for power.

Peace comes as God's gift when we seek it in our conversations with the Holy One—when we take time to receive it. *Let it be true, O God! Let it be true!* Relax and receive it.

Concern for peace clearly goes far beyond personal peace within our individual lives. World peace and divine protection of endangered people are certainly huge issues. Sincere and constant prayer that reaches beyond ourselves is an obvious task and is our ever present responsibility. Have no doubt, it can make a crucial difference in the complexion of the world scene. We must not fail in this charge.

In a prayer, attributed to Saint Francis of Assisi, we are given helpful thoughts to ponder: "Make me a channel of your peace. Where there is hatred, let me bring love. Where there offense, let me bring pardon. Where there is discord, let me bring union. Where there is despair, let me bring hope. Where there is darkness, let me bring light. Where there is sadness, let me bring joy." That is how peace happens! It is God's gift that flows into us, giving us rest, then through us into the many cracks and crevasses of the world.

Let there be peace on earth, and let it begin with me. We are the very ones God uses to help give birth to peace. We are the midwives. We do not create peace, but we do assist in its birth. It comes not as a victory but as a gift—first as rest for us, then as hope and healing for the world.

As we open ourselves to receive this miraculous peace, it sets into motion an incredible cycle of escalating peace and gratitude.

Spiritual Growth and Development

We are all spiritual beings because we are created in the *image* of God who is spirit. Spiritual growth is the process of learning to live as a spiritual being. This process does not come naturally but is an exciting journey that inherently has the power to transform our lives from the inside out. This journey has the potential to awaken our spirits and make them the dominant force in our daily living—to change our perspective of everything, as if we are given corrective lenses to see things as they really are for the first time ever.

This spiritual journey begins when we allow the Spirit of God who dwells within us to become the dominant force and begin taking over the control of our lives—to move into the driver's seat, moving us out of that stressful position.

When we wake up each morning our first thoughts should not be what do I need to do today but I wonder what God will do with me today. Where will God lead me? What will God have me do? How will everything I normally do have a different meaning?

Our daily morning prayer might well become a simple statement: Thank you, God, for inviting me into your day, giving me the joy of having you dwell within me, leading me in everything that I do. Grant me the willingness and courage to embark upon this journey, wherever it might take me.

This journey of our spirits being led by the Spirit of God within us is truly a new way of seeing and experiencing everything.

A case in point is seeing the difference between being grateful for God's helping us through hard times versus being awakened to the truth that this newly energized relationship with God is the way all life with God is designed to be lived. Life is first and foremost about our connection to God. Our spirits are designed to be infused by God's Spirit. We are lifted above the din to live a new life with a new purpose and new perspective. We have a new take on life—a new reason to get out of bed each morning. God is no longer just a companion but becomes our entire reason for being.

It often takes a trip through pain for this significant transformation to take place. We must not be afraid of pain or hard times. It is not just something to get through and beyond.

Rather, it is an invaluable opportunity to experience as never before the unyielding and relentless divine love and mercy and engage with the Holy One in a relationship that has new and exciting dimensions. Darkness and pain are the very stuff of spiritual growth and development—the cocoon.

Navigating Life

Through the many years of growing up and maturing, we struggle to get a fix on what is going on and how we are fitting into the scheme of things. Our inquisitiveness is often acute and leads us in many directions through the years. We persistently ask ourselves where we want our lives to go and how successful are we at this moment.

We measure our progress by our own perception of others' perceptions of us. Furthermore, we are constantly sorting through the myriad possibilities that lie before us in life. Where are we headed?

We worry about ourselves and how well or how poorly we feel we are doing—how successfully we are navigating life and managing ourselves in this process. Concern for our personal growth and development lurks like an omnipresent shadow in the recesses of our minds—sometimes lightly, sometimes heavily. Living is stimulating, to say the least. It is like climbing a rock wall—requiring that we develop skills, maintain courage, employ determination, and cling to hope.

Life can be depressing and overwhelming. At times it seems like a smooth paved road with a few scattered pot holes; at other times it seems like one big pot hole—a sink hole.

There are many human stories of people who overcome trials and difficulties of many sorts—loss, injury, illness, tragedy—any one of which has the potential to put a stiff foot on our necks.

Humankind has mustered strong resistance in order to keep going and not be defeated. Sometimes it is pure grit. Sometimes it is astounding cleverness. Sometimes it is someone's help. Sometimes nothing seems to make a difference.

How can we confront this long-term challenge of living and not only survive but succeed?

It should be no surprise to us that the one who put us here in the first place, Almighty God, has followed up on the original handiwork and is available to assist us throughout this living process.

In many, and often subtle, ways God says to us over and over, Let me assist you as you navigate your way through life. Let me help you with your decision-making, for that is one key to a satisfying life. Since I know the ropes, let me partner with you. I created the system and know how it works so I can be of great assistance to you. Consider taking me on board and thereby gain access to my expertise. It might not occur to you that living your life without my participation is like canoeing without a paddle.

The more we rely upon God, the more directed and energized our lives become. It comes down to who is going to be the CEO. God has volunteered. It is wise for us to put our egos and fears to rest and accept this incredible offer.

Prayer: OK, God. I think I hear you. You are on! Where do we go from here? Lead me! Direct me! Be my partner. Come into my life today; come in to stay; come close to me. Let me feel your presence. Help me navigate life.

Discovering What Your Life Is About

Picking raspberries is a fun task. *One into the bucket—one into my mouth!* A great metaphor for living. Life is indeed a fun task. It's great and fully worth living. But what is it all about? Has it just happened to us? Did we just appear on the scene? Is it solely for us to enjoy, or is there more to our existence?

Many people conclude life is merely what has happened and still is happening to us. Without asking any questions about why or what it is all about, they proceed to live sans any significant mission, or if there is a vision, it is centered around themselves with little or no outlook. What's in it for me?

Ranking where we are at the top of the created order on earth, and given the ability to think, reason, and imagine, it should be obvious that there is some agenda that accompanies our existence. Simply being here should raise at least some philosophical questions if not faith issues. Why? Why? Why?

Beyond philosophical questions there are major spiritual questions that obviously need to be asked. Are there important reasons for my being here?

If you are reading this, you obviously have some concern for your life's purpose beyond living it solely for yourself. Like picking raspberries, there is the immediate delight of eating as you pick. However, with bucket in hand you know there is more to it than the immediate satisfaction. There is an agenda. There is a mission.

What then is your life all about? From a spiritual perspective life is to be seen as having a specific and unique mission for each individual. That means you are here not just for your own agenda but also to do something specific. It may not be grandiose and might seem quite ordinary to you, the reason being it is not extremely difficult for you because of your special talents. God has given you talents as unique gifts for you to use in fulfilling your specific mission in life.

Your calling in life is for you to discover and use your unique abilities to fulfill your mission.

Because you have been given these talents there is never any room for arrogance or boasting, or even feeling superior. You are merely doing what your life has been designed to do however impressive or unimpressive it might be. Whatever it turns out to be, if you pursue it, it will be satisfying for you. You are who you are and how you are, not because of how you have made yourself but because you have taken seriously your search for what your life is all about.

Enjoy picking and eating life's raspberries, but don't forget why you have a bucket.

Discovering God's Purpose for Your Life

It is unusual for us at an early age to become concerned about God's purpose for our lives. If the question ever arises it is most likely to surface when we are mature, having successfully passed through many stages of human development.

Our younger years are consumed by more personal agendas—appearance, friends, school, sports, career, success— all of which seem to be in such constant flux. During those difficult formative years, emotional survival demands consummate attention. We need much encouragement and a stable environment to come out of this tumbling machine safely. Few people would choose to go through these early years again.

At whatever point one begins to feel life is more manageable and promising, it is appropriate and timely to begin the inquiry into God's purpose for one's life.

If we look back over our years of development, whether they have been placid or tumultuous, we should begin to recognize God's handprint on our lives. It should become apparent, although slowly, God has been guiding us through the maze—protecting us, guiding us—for some purpose. Our lives have not been lived as if on an undefined open range but with guiding direction and purpose—God's purpose.

Our maturation should suggest to us that not only are we special to God but we are also uniquely gifted to fulfill some specific mission. The big challenge is discovering that mission—God's purpose.

Discovering it may be simple and straightforward, or it may be complex and require special preparation. It may become obvious or it may remain temporarily hidden, but it is there to discover.

Learning that God does indeed have a special purpose in life for each of us can be quite consoling after years of wondering and searching for the meaning of life. Discovering God's purpose for us and pursuing it is what brings satisfaction and a sense of fulfillment.

Unfortunately, it is easy for us to lose our direction and get off course—missing the goal. Such misfortune can bring confusion and disappointment. If this occurs, it is as difficult to get back on track as it is to get a wrecked train back on track. It can be done but only by God, who is fully equipped to cope with our human train wrecks.

We will know clearly when we are on track. It can be ascertained by how successful we are at making a positive difference in people's lives and how clear we are about helping make the world a better place for all of God's people. That is our individual and corporate mission and *God's* purpose for us.

Our GPS is persistent prayer and faithful meditation—getting closer and closer to the Holy One.

Living on a Higher Plane

Many highly religious people are stuck on a level of living that keeps them in a constant state of struggle. Alas, struggle has become the norm for even religious people.

Struggle describes one's response to life's stressful situations. There are those persons, however, who have either been gifted directly by God or who have learned through exploration that one does not necessarily have to endure a life of struggle.

Life lived securely connected to God is lifted to a higher plane and is a far distance from the ordinary. We do not need merely to trudge through each day. We can instead glide through whatever the day brings by living on a higher plane. Hydroplaning comes to mind with its rising above the water where friction is greatly reduced. We can transcend the friction of ordinary living by utilizing the spiritual gifts available to us to live an extraordinary life.

Unfortunately, far too many people of faith fail to cash in their *faith chips*, allowing them to accumulate unused. These people may be productive, happy, and seemingly satisfied with their lots in life but still not filled with peace and joy. Peace and joy come with living on a higher plane. Life can take on a glow that energizes us in ways no dietary supplement can produce.

How do we capitalize on this promise by God? How do we engage life's hydroplane possibility?

It is basic and simple. We alter our way of perceiving the everyday things we do. We engage them as opportunities rather than chores. We give them different labels. We redefine difficulties as opportunities for growth rather than mud holes we must somehow get through. We invite God to transform the way we have looked at life—allowing it to become a scene of opportunity. Old chores become new challenges filled with unforeseen promise.

God promises not only to make us into new creatures—a whale of a bailout—but also to cast a new light on all of life so it glows with peace and joy. No longer are we confined to a flat-screen existence—life on this higher plane is in 3-D, perhaps even 4-D.

This comes about when we begin to get more serious about our relationship with God and move closer. It takes some palpable commitment to this process and an openness to new possibilities with the Holy One. The sky is the limit!

Surrendering

Getting to know God on a new level and learning to love God *more dearly* is surely the most exciting and rewarding life process in which we can engage.

Loving God with our whole hearts, minds, and souls is a familiar concept and has been designated as the most important law to have written on our hearts. Loving God is an orientation of our spirits toward God. It is also a commitment to pursue this love in some form of an interactive relationship with the Holy One.

Most of us know something about love and have experienced it with people who have been meaningful and important to us. It is a motivating force that brings out the best in us. We love and are loved. It is a most gratifying way to live and one that brings happiness—even joy—into our lives, and most likely to the ones we love. Deep love smites us and knocks us off our props. It causes us to lose our senses and sends us twirling. We are unleashed from reason, abandon good sense, and focus exclusively on the one with whom we have come to love. If this love is returned by the object of our affection, we are caught up in a state of ecstasy beyond description.

Our wills become engaged and we shift our time and attention toward the object of our love. Our thoughts are consumed; our imagination runs untethered. Our hearts palpitate. Our sole desire is to be with the one we love with this newly discovered love.

We have been created to have these feelings, and we are free to feel them deeply. We surrender to them, and we allow them to completely redirect our lives.

This overwhelming experience is one we can also experience with God. If and when we do, we begin to get a sense of what creation is all about. We begin to develop an awareness of how life is designed to be lived within God's great plan.

We give up trying to fabricate a life on our own that has held promise but has not delivered. We become so awed by the Holy One that we surrender—little by little—until it becomes unconditional. It is then we want, more than any worldly success we have ever sought, to live in the presence of the Holy One who has won our affection. Surrendering our lives to God is not something we decide but find ourselves doing when we learn to love our gracious creator with our whole heart, mind, and soul.

Amen! May It Be So! The Gift of God's Spirit

In the total religious scheme of things, spirituality is unique. While our initial religious experience is filled with what we believe about God, faith, life, other people, and the world, all of which are important, spirituality focuses on one single matter— God's relationship with us. Spirituality focuses upon that vital hook-up that God has established with us and the far-reaching ramifications of this connection.

Unfortunately, it is necessary to defend spirituality against the frequent criticism that it is too focused on our feelings. Spirituality is not about our feelings but about *awareness*— awareness of God's immediate presence in our world and within our innermost beings.

It all begins with God. The promise of God to His people of old and to us has always been that we are never alone. God is with us. Emmanuel! That part of the scenario never changes. What does change is our *awareness* of his omnipresence. Thus, it is vital for us to consider the matter of our *awareness* of God's existing presence in our lives. It is this *awareness* we need to sharpen if we wish to grow and mature spiritually.

There are several levels of awareness. One is superficial, illustrated by a hastily offered thanks at a meal. A second is moving, which we might experience as we listen to music. A third is psychological such as deep sorrow at the loss of a loved one. A fourth is serenity that is present when life is stormy. At this fourth level, we become aware that God's Spirit is dwelling within us, subduing our fear and anxiety while sparking calm and deeply felt joy.

As with all relationships, enhancing our relationship with God takes time, attention, patience, commitment, and tenacious hope.

The method is conversation. We might struggle with praying on the first three levels. The fourth level is simple. We scarcely say anything. We simply bask in the warmth and love of God's presence, trusting the ultimate promise that the Holy One lives and dwells within us creating joy and gratitude. It is life's most satisfying state of being.

Healing Comes When God's Spirit Moves Freely Within Us

We can be so completely focused on our bodies and physical lives that our spiritual nature gets neglected, if not completely ignored. God is quite interested in our physical well-being having given us our bodies. They are holy temples in which our spirits dwell. We are charged to maintain these temples as sacred gifts. God remains involved with us in this lifelong project. The Holy Spirit mysteriously lives within us and when given the freedom to function nourishes and heals our bodies.

The Spirit brings divine energy to strengthen and cleanse us. The promise is to make us whole (holy). That which disrupts the free-flowing function of the Spirit within our bodies is dispelled. Given the thousands of bodily functions that can go awry and create physical problems, there are very few that fail us, although they can and do confront us with serious and life-threatening illness. Eventually, our bodies do wear out—these temples do crumble—having served their temporary purpose of housing our spirits.

In the meantime, while physical life plays out, the divine will is for us to be healthy and able to fulfill God's purpose in our lives. We are to carry out God's plan to manage the plantation (creation) and have it produce those necessary products that are propagated to nourish and sustain all life. The agenda for us who have been created in God's image is to care for one another in ways that bring healing into the lives of all of God's people. This can occur when God's Spirit moves freely within us.

We are aware of our awesome failure to fulfill our assignment when we see the horrible conditions in which so many people seem destined to live. Our task—our purpose in life—is to uplift all humankind. It is a test to determine if we are able to free ourselves of obsessive self-worship and, with clarity of purpose, care for God's people everywhere.

Life is designed to be filled with peace and joy. Peace and joy come to us when we bring it to others. This mystical interconnection evolves naturally as we allow God's Spirit to move freely within us.

Mindfulness Throughout the Day

We who desire to be on a spiritual journey are always searching for methods we can employ to assist us on a daily basis to keep on track. Perhaps we have made commitments to pursue our spirituality more diligently, only to have it slip away in the busyness of the day. This happens to everyone.

Following are suggestions to assist us in our endeavor to become more faithful and mature in the fulfillment of our own commitments. As with any maturing process, it takes discipline and practice to develop. In this case, it takes an effort to remain mindful of what it is we truly desire for our lives. Spiritual maturity comes as a result of relentless *desire* to pursue God's will for us, however faltering our efforts may be.

It is helpful to be mindful that success in this pursuit does *not* come in direct proportion to our own efforts. Rather, it comes as a *gift* from God, and it usually comes slowly, and often is apparent only in retrospect.

As we pursue this spiritual journey with God, one requisite is being open to new and inexplicable experiences. It is important to remember we will live within a healthy degree of mystery. Understanding is scanty—acceptance is vital.

With the stage now set we are ready to become the actors on stage. What then is our script? How do we act out our role?

The first step will be a *perception shift.* This is fundamental. We need to begin seeing each day in a new way. Although we might continue to do the same things within the day, now we will do them with a mindfulness that they are not just daily chores but are all a part of our day with God. We give each day that special context, labeling it *God's day.* The important cue is understanding we live in *God's day,* rather than inviting God into our day. This is a highly significant *perceptual shift.* It is key to remaining mindful.

The second step in this daily process is to reestablish that unique perception at various times throughout the day. This is necessary because the initial perception shift slips away unless it is renewed. How do we prevent this?

First, we should begin each day with a quiet time, perhaps when we first awaken while still lying in bed. Memorize John Baillie's prayer and pray it slowly and thoughtfully:

O Holy Spirit of God, visit now this soul of mine, and tarry within it until eventide. Inspire all my thoughts. Pervade all my imaginations. Suggest all my decisions. Lodge in my will's most inward citadel and order all my doings. Be with me in my silence and in my speech, in my haste and in my leisure, in company and in solitude, in the freshness of the morning and in the weariness of the evening; and give me grace at all times to rejoice in Thy mysterious companionship.

Praying this prayer will orient our approach to the day from its beginning.

As noted earlier, this aura will fade as we get busy. Consequently, it is imperative to reestablish that *perceptual* shift of living in God's day and to thank God for inviting us into this special day. *Thank you, O Holy One, for inviting me into your day to experience the joy of being with you in everything I do.*

Quiet time, whether long or short, creates a necessary break in what we are doing and provides an opportunity to reorient our focus. The length of time spent in quiet time is not as important as the break itself.

In these brief moments we need to refocus on the bigger picture and be mindful that we are living within God's plan.

Maintaining Your Spiritual Health

Like many things in life, setting a spiritual direction and staying on course are two very different experiences. One could compare it to losing weight and keeping off the excess pounds. It is difficult to stay on course with the many distractions that surround us and occupy our attention. However, finding a way to maintain our spiritual health is worth whatever it takes to do it.

Following are some suggestions that hopefully will be helpful in maintaining your spiritual health. It is common to experience some lapses along the way. Whenever that happens, and it will, we should start the very same day as if nothing has gone awry. Forgive yourself.

One very helpful tool is choosing a spiritual companion who desires to be on a similar journey. It could be a partner, spouse, friend, or perhaps a new friend who holds this same spiritual outlook. Set regularly scheduled times for sharing the values along with apparent hopes and failures. Stay positive and don't dwell on failure or weaknesses. Pray together. Get God involved.

Develop an *attitude of gratitude.* This attitude should become second nature and take up residency in the forefront of our awareness. We need to get into the habit of looking at our blessings, which are countless, and consciously give thanks for them time and time again. We will soon begin to recognize many more of these blessings. Some of them have been taken for granted for too long, for example, the gift of our minds, which work amazingly well in spite of our inability to remember things we want desperately to remember. Name to yourself some of the things your mind has done well. Give thanks. Once again stay positive. Keep your glass half full, never half empty.

Whenever you do feel grateful for something, put your mind on pause to say thank you to God. As these pauses of gratitude accumulate throughout the day, you will be amazed how this keeps you on course.

Keep tabs on your mental activity. Our minds, while being wonderful and amazing gifts, have a tendency to run rampantly. This can be both creative and wasteful. Check in with some self-examination every so often in your day to tell your mind what to think about. Choose routine things you do as checkpoints throughout the day that will remind you to refocus. Focus the boundless energy of your mind on something that you wish to pursue. Keep it on a leash. Don't let it run unchecked. If there is something you wish to have your mind work on, tell yourself what it is and ask God to partner in the effort. Then you can let your mind out on an extend-a-leash.

Direct your awareness toward how much of life's everyday experiences have spiritual components. We mostly pass through these experiences on our way to somewhere else in our thoughts and fail to sense the spiritual component. For example, drinking water is a most ordinary act, but it can become much more than that. It can be a wonderful moment, for not only does water keep our bodies healthy, it is also the same substance with which we are baptized and adopted into God's family. It has a huge spiritual component. We need only to train ourselves to recognize how spiritual many ordinary things can be if only we make the connection.

Let one of your daily prayer petitions center around surrendering your will to God's will. God can transform your will into his will. Remember the Lord's Prayer and consciously repeat it. *Your will be done on earth as it is in heaven* (and let it begin with me). Pray throughout each day. *Show me your Holy*

Will and empower me to do it. Trust that it will happen. Recognize it and celebrate it when it does.

We are encouraged to pray without ceasing. This calls not for continuous prayer but for the maintenance of a persistent prayerful attitude. It entails an awareness that we live in God's time, not our own. All time is God's time and we are in it together with the Holy One. God invites us in. Every minute of every day God is with us. We can chat with God, even under our breath, about everything that is going on in our lives. In so doing we constantly give thanks and ask for guidance. What do I need to be doing? Guide me to where you want me to be. Awaken in me the awareness of your desire for me. Give me the courage to carry out your will, which is always best for me.

There are times when our minds are off on an errand while at the same time we feel a need to refocus on our spiritual well-being. It can be difficult to make the switch we feel we need to make. A wonderful tool for helping with this switch is the use of devotional material. Reading spiritual devotional material hastens the transition from the mundane to the spiritual. Regular use of this book as devotional material can serve in that role.

Although the mundane has its rightful place, it does manifest its maximum value when given a spiritual context. The world in which we live is the stage on which our spiritual lives are played.

Spiritual maturity, while at times seeming to be elusive, is certainly an ideal. In fact, all of life should be spent in pursuing and developing that maturity. We can grow toward it and reap its rewards. Unfortunately, we cannot keep ourselves on track at all times. We are self-centered creatures constantly in need of God's grace and forgiveness. We need the guidance of the Holy Spirit to empower us to carry out any of this function. Yet, the truth is that with God's help we can grow into much of this and experience unbelievable joy in our increasing success.

The key to maintaining our spiritual health is prayer and meditation in different forms. Those two sides of the same coin are indispensable. Spirituality is simply staying connected to God and allowing God the opportunity to mold us into people who love God with our whole hearts, minds, and spirits, and who are empowered to love all others as we learn to love ourselves.

Starting Over Again—and Again

Create in me a clean heart, O God, and put a new and right spirit in me. According to some Biblical scholars, these are the words of King David, who had wronged his closest friend, Nathan, and was desperately seeking forgiveness from God. He was searching for a new chance at a better life unencumbered by his guilt. David's additional words denoting his profound sorrow and confession were, *Against you and you only, O God, have I sinned and done this evil in your sight.*

We may or may not at this point in our own lives feel the angst and agony of some terrible evil taking control of us as David apparently experienced. Hopefully, that is not the case with us. Nevertheless, we know full well that we are not without sin. Yet, we tend to modify and mute the severity of our immoral thoughts and deeds in an attempt not to be overly harsh on ourselves. But evil lurks within us relentlessly. There are no timeouts. We are always exposed—always vulnerable. Our best efforts will not keep us unstained. Unfortunately, it is a part of who we are and how we are. After accepting our sinful nature, we put ourselves at God's mercy and ask for help as David did. We should stand in awe of David, who either had the outright courage or was led by God's Holy Spirit to seek divine help.

Create in me a clean heart, O God. Clean me up. I am unable to stay on the straight and narrow way. In this condition I do not despair, although I am saddened. I do not despair because God is constantly in the process of cleansing my heart—cleaning up my messy life. This is an ongoing process. Where I cannot change my own heart, God does. That is the wonder of this spiritual journey. God does create in me a clean heart—again and again. I am remodeled every day so that every day and every moment is new. My spirit, the heart and core of who I am in my very essence, is being remade and renewed constantly.

While I cannot bring this about with my own strength or will, the Holy Spirit works this miracle within me regardless of how far out of bounds I have strayed.

The clear message of the psalmist to us is that there has never been a slowdown in God's effort to make all things new. We are a part of that restoration. As we are given the gift of new life every day, so we bring new life into the world every day. That is God's modus operandi.

The Far Reach of God's Forgiveness

Most of us have heard about forgiveness from many sources for most of our lives. The Lord's Prayer, familiar to many, holds up forgiveness as a most valuable gift. God promises our sins have been forgiven. The verb tense is past perfect, indicating the act has already been completed! Perhaps you have experienced the tremendous relief of having some heavy-duty guilt lifted from you, followed by a magnanimous sense of gratitude.

Unfortunately, most of us tend to be quite cavalier about God's forgiveness. It is not that we do not believe God will and does forgive. The glitch comes because we do not consider the extent to which God is willing to go to forgive us and assure us we have been forgiven. The slate has been wiped clean—there is no residue left unaccounted for, and no trace remains. Forgiveness is complete and permanent. It is of utmost importance for us to assimilate the full extent of this amazing truth!

Our tendency is unconsciously to hang on to shards of our wrongdoing. We have a hard time letting go. We continue to feel some guilt. We allow feelings of self-condemnation to resurface at later dates, bringing phantom burdens back into existence. We find ourselves thinking we have additional responsibility, especially if we repeat the offense, and we often do just that. Particular misdeeds often are habitual. We have great difficulty shaking free of their tentacles.

Rather than succumbing to feelings of failure and picking up guilt, it is incumbent upon us to remind ourselves we are promised complete and continuing forgiveness.

There are no limits to God's far-reaching forgiveness. We cannot repeat a sin so many times that it causes God in disgust to say, *That's it! No more! That is one too many! You have gone too far this time!* God is not as we are—limited in forgiveness resources.

Furthermore, not only is God willing to forgive endlessly, but also this divine gift can be bestowed upon us so we too can continue forgiving those who offend us, far beyond our normal limits. God empowers us to forgive.

Of course, God's gift of unlimited forgiveness is not a license to sin freely but should become a harness to better control our sinful nature. In our confessions we acknowledge we are by nature sinful and unclean and have sinned by thought, word, and deed. Because of our very nature the total control of our sinfulness is impossible. We must prayerfully try to avoid the pit, all the while knowing it is truly beyond our complete control.

A trick we often play on ourselves is to assume some things at which we continue to fail are not actually sinful after all. Of course, we do not have the authority to redefine things in that way, however tempting and convenient it might be. It is much better to admit and confess our failure and receive complete forgiveness, which once and for all cleans the slate.

Receiving forgiveness is a profound spiritual experience.

Openness to Being Changed by God

The mirrors on the passenger side of our cars reflect different size images than do the ones on the driver's side. On the passenger side the images are smaller and look far more distant. For that reason, there is etched on the surface of the mirror these words of warning: *Objects in mirror are closer than they appear.* That is not only a physical reality. It is a spiritual truth. Things are not always as they appear to be. Our perceptions can be inaccurate.

The world is full of false conclusions drawn by people who are obstinately certain they are correct. No discipline is more filled with this sort of misperception than religion. The incidence of people claiming apodictic certainty of their conclusions is perhaps even higher in religious circles than anywhere else. Look at the wide range of religious groups, each holding tenaciously to truth as they perceive it. The number is astounding.

So, where does the real truth lie? Are we correct in our dogma? How can we be certain of what we believe? Better questions might be, How can we develop a process for determining the trustworthiness of our beliefs? How can we learn to know and trust God enough to give up beliefs we hold that are not congruent with what the Holy Spirit teaches us?

Once we move into the realm of the Holy Spirit we quickly become aware that things indeed are not necessarily as they appear to be. If we are willing to allow ourselves to be at the mercy and direction of the Holy Spirit, we must be open to having our perceptions altered.

We begin this process by relinquishing the notion that we are correct in many of our assumptions about life and God as well as ourselves. As we look into a mirror we become aware that what we see is not what we may have imagined ourselves to be. Certainly, we are more than appears on the surface of that glass on the wall. To look into a spiritual mirror is to see ourselves as God sees us. That image becomes one of loveliness and gracefulness, which may not be the way we have seen ourselves. Not only are we loved, we are made truly lovely and lovable by God. God molds us as the potter molds the clay, giving us new form—new life. That is why the Psalmist's prayer is so appropriate for us as we experience this spiritual development: *Create in me a new and right spirit.*

Allowing ourselves to be changed—transformed into someone new—is not an easy choice to make. It may be easy to wish it so but more difficult to let ourselves go into the masterful hands of God and not worry about the outcome of God's handiwork. However, the transformation we experience at God's hands is worth the risk. Whether or not we like the way we are now, we will like ourselves better when God gets finished with our makeover. Let the change begin! Most likely it has already begun.

Grace and Gratitude

Grace is theologically defined as *God's unmerited favor* extended to us. It comes to us because of God's unfathomable love for us and our desperate need for divine acceptance. Grace is a huge gift of incredible measure.

Given even our very best efforts to please God and obey, we still fall short of the mark. By thought, word, and deed we are inescapably sinful beings. Given the testimony and verdict, we are guilty. We deserve to be ostracized by God.

Although God is rightfully offended, the rules are not bent, letting us slide through. Rather, they are superseded by grace. As a result, the insult our failures bring to God is absorbed by God, and instead of punishing us, God covers our failure with a mask of forgiving *grace.*

Our offenses miraculously vanish from God's vision, and we appear as no longer dirty failures but clean and pure children.

We remain aware of our true nature and failures, but God has covered everything from his view, absorbing it into his own being.

At this juncture our task is to relinquish our natural arrogance, accept the gift of forgiveness in its entirety, and allow the graciousness of God to transform our lives—thought, word, and deed.

Grace is a pure gift with no strings attached. It not only sets us entirely free of our guilt, it crushes our egos and the hubris we exude that is as offensive as halitosis. Our natural arrogance is replaced with humility. Our persistent desire to be in charge is replaced by emerging gratitude that divine control is taking over and we do not have to be in charge. Not only are we increasingly aware we have been set free of guilt, but we discover to our amazement, gratitude is growing within us like a green shoot in the springtime—grace and gratitude.

Gratitude is an attitude—an orientation to life whose power produces the true joy we can experience. Gratitude lubricates our passage through life. God's grace is responsible for the conception of gratitude; it is our responsibility and privilege to nourish it, bring it to full term, and give birth to a life motivated by gratitude.

Gratitude is alive within each of us, at least in its initial stage—ovum. The orientation toward its birth has been set in motion. It is our decision and determination that bring it to full term and birth—a new life. It is a fully functioning *attitude of gratitude*, bringing sheer joy to us and through us into the groping, struggling world. Grace is God's magnetic pull that draws us into an awesome closeness.

Discerning God's Will

Countless numbers of people demonstrate little or no interest in either knowing God's will for them or pursuing it. They appear to be concerned solely with pursuing their own wills and wishes. However, the thoughts presented here are directed to those who have become increasingly aware that getting to know and pursuing *God's* will are life's best choices. You have arrived at that conclusion by God's grace and are now seeking ways of discerning God's holy will for you. It is important to give special thanks for this initial nudge.

Perhaps the words of the Lord's Prayer have begun to take on heightened meaning: *Your Kingdom come, your will be done, on earth as in heaven*—especially by me.

As stated earlier, we experience life at its very best when we are in accord with God's will for us. Therefore, discerning God's holy will is an imperative for an enhanced and energized life.

The question frequently arises: How can I be certain that what I think is truly God's will is not just my own will parading in religious garb? This has become a debilitating dilemma for many sincere people. In that context, what we are likely seeking is a higher degree of probability that what comes into our minds is truly God's directive.

Far more important than *certainty* is God's *promise* to guide us. In fact, certainty does not even exist and is merely a mental construct. We need to learn to live by God's promise rather than seeking certainty that what we are thinking is correct. The promise is that we will be guided if we so desire.

The resolution of this dilemma comes with trusting God to reveal His will to us with sufficient clarity. Appropriating this revelation comes with realizing God can make our wills consonant with His divine will by transforming our hearts, minds, and wills.

We tend to use the traditional practice of our particular religious communities as a guide for determining God's will. This is a good place to start, as long as we acknowledge these traditions are often in flux and constantly evolving. They are by no means absolute although certainly worthy of our consideration.

In areas where there is no clear tradition to follow, the situation becomes more complex. There is no road map, no blueprint to guide us. Scripture might be silent on the subject, or even confusing and seemingly contradictory. How then do we discern what is God's will for us without some guideline?

When we are confronted by this sort of situation, we are compelled to trust that God will somehow get through to us in some recognizable fashion. Meanwhile, we should guard against thinking we must perform the right maneuver, utter the right prayer, or put our minds into some exotic mode. All this does is heap massive guilt upon us because we cannot make it happen. We can never figure out God's will for us by our own efforts. God's will is not discoverable by our hot pursuit as if it were hidden or buried under some mass of cover.

All that we need to know or can know does not come from our searching but simply from our openness to God's self-revelation. Thus, our method for discerning God's will for us is to allow God to make it known to us. We do not search—we wait. If we assume that stance, amazing things will happen.

One of the most exciting spiritual experiences we can have is for God to plow and cultivate our minds. This divine action can be disturbing and uncomfortable for a time, but the results are most gratifying. God's Holy Spirit can directly inspire our minds, planting thoughts and ideas. It may seem to us that these ideas and thoughts are our own, but clearly the Holy Spirit is at work. When this occurs, we must free our own spirits from any rational constraints in order to receive and interpret God's message to us.

Our own awakened and sensitized spirits can pick up these signals from the Holy Spirit while our rational minds might remain totally oblivious. Obviously, we need to exercise our spirits in order to sensitize them for this task. We do this by consistently placing our spirits in the divine presence— spending time with the Holy One in quiet time and solitude. This spiritual practice is an ancient one and is amazingly dependable. In fact, it is hazardous to proceed in our actions until we invest devotedly in this particular spiritual practice. Once we pause and involve ourselves in prayerful quiet time, then we can move with the confidence that we are at least under God's direction. It is like hooking up the pull cord before parachuting out of an airplane.

Another aspect of discerning God's will is being aware that God can and often does *infuse* us with his will. In the same manner in which God said to his people he would *write his law upon their hearts,* he can directly infuse us with his will. In a miraculously direct manner his will becomes our will—there is but one will. When this occurs, we no longer have to struggle to discern God's will for us but trust ourselves to proceed because we have been infused with God's will—God's will has become operational within us.

Discernment evokes a gradual and mysterious change in our lives. Unfortunately, this change can lose its grip unless we are constantly in prayer, asking God to maintain this gift of discernment. When this gift remains in place, God's will becomes our way of life. We will still err because evil lurks within us and throughout the world of which we are an integral part. However, as a way of life, opening ourselves to divine inspiration produces life at its very best.

Thy Will Be Done

We have been taught to pray because prayer changes things. We believe it makes a difference or we would not bother to pray. Sometimes the change occurs in what is happening around us or to us. At other times the change occurs within us, altering the way we see things—our perspective. Regardless of how God wishes to make the change, something happens that makes things different—always better in the long run and in God's own time.

Your Kingdom come, your will be done on earth as in heaven. These words that Jesus taught us to use in our praying are perhaps so familiar to us they could have lost their potency. Their potency needs to be reinstated and their power recaptured. If we dwell on these words we will eventually come to the realization that the overarching source of all positive power is God's will. The world is made to operate according to

God's will. Therefore, life for us is at its best when we live in consonance with God's will.

Whenever we seriously come to grips with God's will and pursue it with determination, a whole new agenda for living shows up on the screen. We find ourselves dancing to a different beat. The music we hear in our hearts is no longer the same. Life takes on an unspeakable aura. The bumps from life's potholes are cushioned. Our agendas are less focused on ourselves—our desires and needs—and more focused on loving God with all our hearts, minds, and souls and our neighbors as ourselves.

If we develop a serious desire for pursuing God's will in our lives, we can be certain that something systemic is changing within us. God has without question been instrumental in shifting our lifestyle.

How can we ascertain it is indeed God's will that constitutes a new agenda for our living? We try it out, and if it is valid it will become self-evident—self-validating. We will know in our hearts. It will be self-assuring. As we walk the walk our confidence will increase.

How God makes this happen will forever remain a mystery for us. We do not need to understand. We just need to allow God's will to govern our lives. Once we get into this mode we will never turn back.

Worship—It Is More Than You Might Think

The root meaning of the word *worship* is the condition of *worth.* Thus, the purpose of worship is to acknowledge God's worth, which is far beyond the value of anyone or anything else in existence. This worth puts God in first place. Nothing else comes close to holding this place of honor. God is above all things. Worship in any form is an overt acknowledgment of this worth, a vital act to perform.

If we believe in God as a real and personal higher power without whom we would not even exist, then some sort of acknowledgment should be forthcoming and inevitable. That acknowledgment and response in whatever form it assumes is worship.

Worship can be carried out in private or in public, preferably and inevitably in both.

Private worship shapes the foundation of our faith. It can take many and varied forms. There are countless ways to engage in private worship. We can set apart special times for prayer and devotion that might include the use of printed material, scripture, or words of hymns. This can become an anchor point for your days.

We can also include prayerful pauses throughout the day for quick moments of touching base with God in a more informal—conversational—way. "Thanks, God, that was awesome."

Prayer in any form, if sincere, is the soaring of our spirits to meet with God's own Spirit.

All of this is worship in a private setting, or even in a busy moment during the day. Private worship can be as informal as we wish, always remembering it is what forms the foundation of our faith, but it should in turn be augmented by corporate worship. Neither alone is adequate acknowledgment of God's worth.

Public or corporate worship is consummately more than *going to church.* It should always be our very best effort to honor and venerate God above everything else. God is to hold that first place in not only our personal and family lives but also our corporate life within the church.

That is the special value of corporate or public worship. It should be designed to refocus our attention on the centrality of

God in the world, which we constantly lose sight of in our daily activities. While it is important to have our private devotions as a daily response to refocus our attention on the truth about God, it is equally important that we regularly come together as a community of faith to demonstrate and celebrate before the world this reality of God's boundless worth and express our gratitude for the gift of life and all that makes it worth living.

Throughout the world millions of people gather regularly at designated times to honor the Holy One who has created us, sustains us, protects us, and directs us. Our very existence and hopes are centered on that truth. We, therefore, are inwardly drawn to acknowledge this in some form of worship.

It is with a deep sense of *awe* that we should carry out this high and holy act of corporate worship, and our comportment should reflect this sense of *awe*.

Our corporate worship must always focus on the Holy One and not on ourselves. There should never be the criticism we have all heard: "I didn't get anything out of church today." It is not about getting anything out of the experience; it is about honoring the Holy One with our very best effort. Our role is to praise and honor God and acknowledge what a gift it is to come into this Holy Presence.

This is the reason people in the past, although not so much today, have dressed in their finest clothes when attending worship. They have done that to honor the Holy One. That, of course, is a personal choice. Unfortunately, dressing can in itself become idolatrous. It has been known to get out of hand, especially at Easter time. It depends upon one's purpose in dressing in the finest. If it is to honor God—great. If it is to draw attention to one's self—not so great. Ultimately dress is totally insignificant as long as it does not distract from the centrality of the Holy One.

If we acknowledge God is truly the One who creates and sustains us, then worship becomes automatic. Not to worship is to ignore God, who stands with us always. The form of worship is our choice. Failure to worship is more than forgetting to say thank you—it is a grievous blunder.

Worship has more to do with life than we might think! If carried out in reverence it not only pleases God but also enriches our lives and enhances our relationship with the Holy One.

Stress—Good and Bad

Much is currently being written about the potentially damaging power of stress in our lives, and ways to deal with it. It has become a highly touted issue in many arenas including medicine, psychology, business, fitness, addiction, and spirituality. Stress has established significant beachheads in numerous dimensions of our society. We are all familiar with its pervasive power, having experienced its effects firsthand. Damage control has moved to front and center.

Because stress can be such an insidious threat to our overall well-being, it is imperative to come to grips with it in a firm, positive manner. An enlightened spiritual response can be most therapeutic.

Initially, as a way of getting a handle on the issue, we can begin by ascribing specific meanings to two terms. First is the term *pressure*. Pressure, as we use it here, is what we feel pushing against us from the outside world. It may come from work, family, relationships, financial status, health, or countless other situations. It may be that our car broke down; we lost our job; our credit cards are maxed out or compromised; we have too much to do and not enough time to do it. All of these examples are *pressures* from the outside world in which we live.

The second word to which we will ascribe particular meaning is *stress*. Stress, as used here, is our personal response to this outside pressure. Stress is the way we gear up to deal with the pressure we are feeling. We push back.

At the outset we need to be clear that a certain amount of stress is essential for our survival. It protects us from danger. Similar to many other human conditions it is basically positive. It becomes a problem only when it is excessive and disproportionate to the existing pressure. It becomes destructive when it overcompensates. Unfortunately, too often that is the case. Some people push back with massive effort regardless of the degree of pressure exerted on them.

The intensity of our response to pressure is our responsibility. While we may not be able to control the outside pressure, the stimulus, we can control our response to it. Damage control is our personal responsibility. Exercise, deep breathing, yoga, meditation, and diet have all been used to control our *stress*. All are helpful.

However, most often overlooked as an available control mechanism for stress is God-power. A spiritual response to pressures we feel coming from many directions is a most powerful and effective resource. It can be no less than miraculous.

While it is important for us to do all we can to change the things that create pressure, we must realize there are situations we cannot change but must confront. Many conditions create pressure that exceeds our ability to cope. It is, therefore, critical for our well-being to engage God-power. We have ready access to this unlimited power that can be utilized in dealing with taxing situations.

Our daily practice should include staying in close touch with God. When that is in place, accessing God's endless power for our daily living becomes a natural resource for *stress* management. We need to turn over to God everything that is excessively stressful. We do the work to change things, but we turn to God to manage the stress.

Life: Death in Remission

Huge strides have been made in increasing our understanding of the basics of physical life and how we can maintain and extend it. Consequently, the length and quality of human life have been increased dramatically. We live considerably longer than our ancestors, and in many ways better.

While we have gained more control over the length and conditions of human life, our knowledge is still severely limited. We have not come up with a way to remove death from the equation. We live longer and better, but we still die. Life seems to be death in remission. We are grateful for life, but in the end we must give it up.

While we have gained extensive knowledge about how to extend and enrich life, when it comes to death, we know very little about it. Death confronts us abruptly with an immovable wall, blocking out all information about what is on the other side. We know far more about living than we do about dying, which is the way it is designed to be.

At this moment we are alive and need to focus on life, although we do it with acute awareness of its temporary nature. It can be helpful for us to see life from that perspective. It is temporary.

Nevertheless, life stands out in bold relief to death, with death being the backdrop for all of life—life always being lived in cautious defiance of death. Sometimes that struggle between life and death is traumatic and intense. At other times it is easy and joyful with momentous success of life as a grace note.

Life does not exist or evolve by happenstance but by deliberate intent of the Holy One. We are the beneficiaries, being gifted with this fabulous opportunity to live and move and have our being on this exotic earth.

How blessed we are to have this gift of life. As long as we have it—every day, every hour—it is pure gift! It is a temporary *remission from death.* As long as it lasts we must spend the time celebrating it and in gratitude making a difference in God's world.

Our lives are lived most joyfully when we catch on to the reason we are here in the first place, e.g., to be with and bring joy to our creator, and while we enjoy its pleasures, enable others to have more joyful lives.

Viewing life as a remission from death puts into perspective the nature of the awesome gift of life and the urgency of living every day as if it were the last one we have.